ROADS
AND TUNNELS

Michael Pollard

Belitha Press

First published in Great Britain in 1996 by
Belitha Press Limited
London House, Great Eastern Wharf
Parkgate Road, London SW11 4NQ

Designer: Hayley Cove
Editor: Christine Hatt
Illustrators: Kevin Maddison / BEEHIVE Illustrations
Picture research: Diana Morris
Consultant: Conor Murphy and Gerry Kelly

ISBN 1 85561 510 X

Printed in Spain

British Library Cataloguing in Publication Data
CIP data for this book is available from the British Library.

Photographic credits
Balfour Beatty: 27 top. Mary Evans Picture Library: 25 top.
Guildhall Library, Corporation of London: 37 top.
Robert Harding Picture Library: 5 bottom.
Hulton Deutsch: 19 top. Illustrated London News Picture Library: 24 bottom.
Ironbridge Gorge Museum Trust: 37 bottom.
Mansell Collection: 18 top. Photri: 21 top, 21 bottom, 38.
Q.A. Photos: 27 bottom. Rex Features Ltd: 7, 30 top SIPA.
Tony Stone Images: 4 Robin Smith, 16 Julian Calder.
Zefa: 5 top Streichan, 39.

The publisher would like to thank Paul Hollands
for providing the diagram on page 14.

Words in **bold** appear in the glossary on pages 46 and 47.

Contents

T13395

Roads

On a map, a road looks like a coloured line stretching across the land. The map does not show how roads are carefully engineered to avoid sharp bends, or how **embankments** and **cuttings** are used to make roads more level.

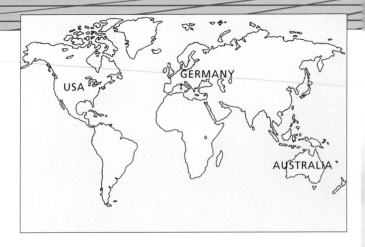

Building in layers

A road that was simply laid over the surface of the ground would soon begin to break up. Roads are built up in layers to make them strong enough to take the constant pounding of heavy traffic.

The road 'cake'

If you could cut a slice of road, you would find that it looks like a many-layered cake. Cables for electricity and telephones, as well as layers of road-making materials, are all laid under the road surface.

Stuart Highway Factfile ▲

Location:	Australia
From:	Darwin, Northern Territory
To:	Adelaide, South Australia
Length:	3250 km
Built:	Early 1940s

The Stuart Highway – named after one of the first European explorers of Australia's outback – existed as a track before the 1940s. During the Second World War, the road was paved to make it suitable for military use.

The Cologne-Bonn Autobahn (motorway) was the first of Germany's high-speed roads. It was rebuilt in the 1950s.

Cologne-Bonn Autobahn Factfile ▶

Location:	Germany
From:	Cologne
To:	Bonn
Length:	32 km
Built:	Early 1930s

Making the roadbed

Hidden from sight underneath the surface is the road's foundation, called the roadbed. This is the bare earth or rock on which the road will be built. The land is bulldozed or blasted with explosives to make cuttings. Then the layers of the road are built on top of the bed.

Interstate 80 Factfile ▼

Location:	USA
From:	Fort Lee, New Jersey
To:	Oakland Bay Bridge, California
Length:	5000 km
Built:	Early 1960s

Getting ready

Modern roads between towns and cities are built for high-speed traffic, and everything is done to make them as easy and safe to use as possible. When a length of road has been built, it is equipped with many aids to drivers, including direction and warning signs, cat's-eyes, lane markings, lighting and emergency telephones.

Interstate 80 is part of a 69 000 km network of multiple-lane highways. Drivers travel the highway without meeting a single traffic light.

STEP BY STEP

In this space on each double page we show you a stage in the building of an imaginary road tunnel. The sequence starts here and ends on page 39.

1 Before a tunnel is planned, **geologists** dig **boreholes** to find out what kind of ground lies on the route.

Choosing the route

Before the route for a new road is chosen, planners and engineers will draw detailed maps of the area. They will consider several routes before making a decision.

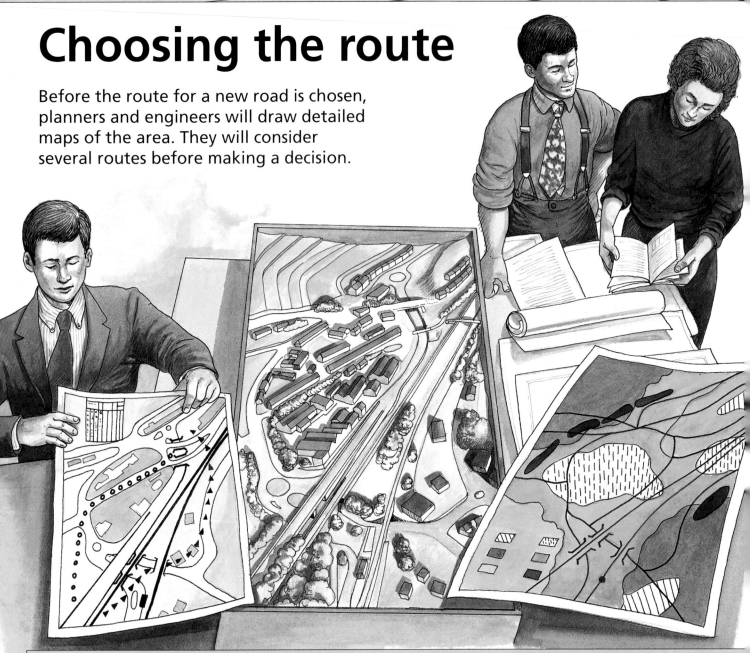

The first stages

The planning of a new road starts years before it is built. The first subject the planners have to think about is how much traffic is likely to use the road. Will it be a **dual carriageway**? How many lanes of traffic will it need? Where are junctions needed with other roads? Planners must also decide where bridges or tunnels are needed, either to carry the new road or to carry existing roads or railways across it.

Keeping costs down

Planners next work out a possible route and inspect it closely on maps and on the site. Geologists often make boreholes to test the soil or rock underneath. The road should avoid marshy ground if possible, because this might cause drainage or structural problems. The smallest possible number of cuttings, embankments, bridges and tunnels must be used because they add hugely to the cost.

Planning ahead

It is not only planners who have an interest in the building of a new road. People living close by may be disturbed by the noise of traffic, or the route may cross areas of scientific importance, such as the habitat of a rare species of bird.

Consulting the public

Plans are made public so that anyone interested in the route knows when the building is due to start and how long it will take to complete the road. Sometimes there is a public enquiry to decide if the road should be built or not.

Protesters sometimes occupy planned road-building sites to try to prevent work starting.

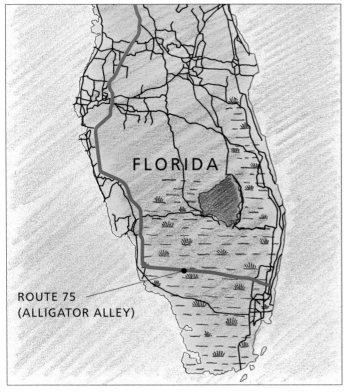

FLORIDA

ROUTE 75 (ALLIGATOR ALLEY)

In Florida, USA, Route 75 runs down the west coast avoiding most of the swampland.

Curves and slopes

The ideal route is one with some gentle curves but no tight bends, and some gentle slopes but no steep ones. Cuttings and embankments may be needed to avoid slopes that are too steep. Curves and slopes allow the road to blend in more easily with the surrounding countryside. They also provide variety, which helps to keep drivers alert. But curves and slopes must be designed so that drivers can see far enough ahead to be able to brake safely if necessary.

STEP BY STEP

2 Once they are ready to start work, geologists examine the rockface closely to find out where to place explosives.

Making a start

The first sign that work is about to start on a new road is the sight of **surveyors** mapping out the route on the ground with marker posts.

The bulldozer pushes away rocks and earth, trees and bushes.

SURVEYOR

THEODOLITE

MARKER POST

Site scenes

Soon the site is invaded by an army of earth-moving equipment – bulldozers, excavators, scrapers and compactors. **Survey stations** are set up so that the surveyors can make constant checks to see that the work is going according to plan. These checks will continue until the road is completed. A special surveying instrument, called a **theodolite**, is used to measure slopes and levels.

Clearing the way

The road-building gangs work on one section of the road at a time, moving along the route in stages. Machines scrape away the soil to prepare a surface in the shape of the new road. Trees, rocks and any other obstructions, such as fences, are removed. If the road has to cut through high ground, any suitable soil and rock removed for the cutting is kept for use where an embankment is needed.

Forming the roadbed

Gradually the line of the road appears as a brown stripe across the countryside. This is the roadbed, which is rolled and **compressed** to make a firm foundation. The top of the roadbed is **cambered**. This means that the centre is higher than the sides so that water can drain away. Where the road curves, the roadbed slopes towards the inside of the curve, so that vehicles can grip the road more easily. When the roadbed is finished, the next stage of building can begin.

Cuttings are **excavated** to take roads through hills and mountains. This makes the slope of the road less steep and easier for traffic to travel along. A cutting also helps drivers to see the road ahead clearly.

Road-builders use a variety of scrapers and compactors to prepare the roadbed. Work continues day and night, using floodlights after dark.

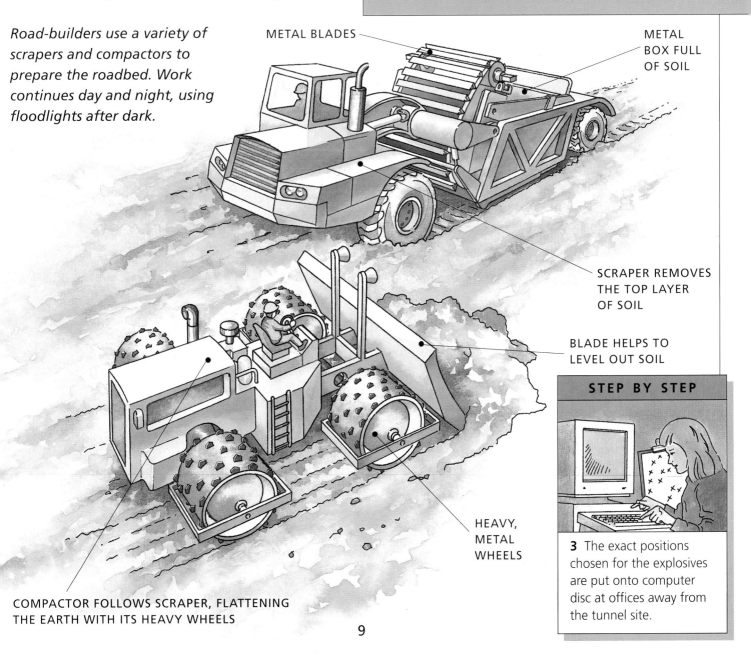

METAL BLADES

METAL BOX FULL OF SOIL

SCRAPER REMOVES THE TOP LAYER OF SOIL

BLADE HELPS TO LEVEL OUT SOIL

HEAVY, METAL WHEELS

COMPACTOR FOLLOWS SCRAPER, FLATTENING THE EARTH WITH ITS HEAVY WHEELS

STEP BY STEP

3 The exact positions chosen for the explosives are put onto computer disc at offices away from the tunnel site.

9

Laying the carriageway

Layers of material built up on the roadbed form the road's **carriageway**. This has to withstand fast-moving, heavy traffic, and must also resist attack by the weather.

HINGED JOINT ALLOWS ARM TO MOVE UP AND DOWN

The excavator digs trenches at the sides of the road to carry the drainage pipes.

CONTROL CABLES

ADJUSTABLE ARM FOR DIGGING

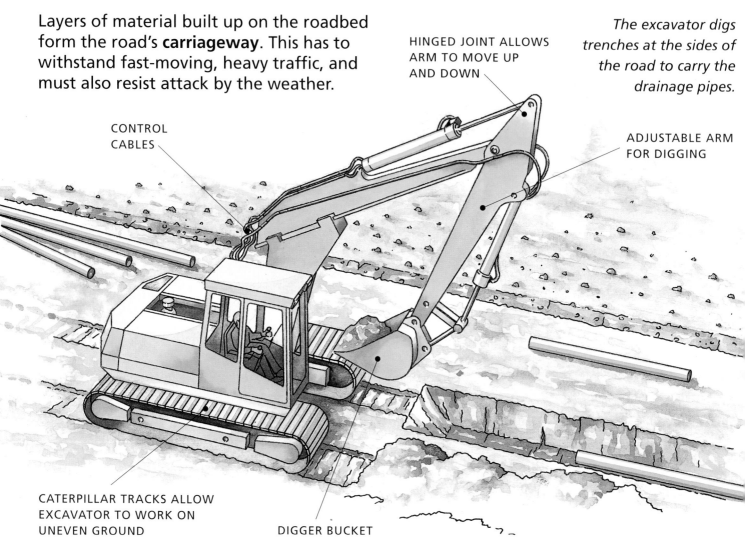

CATERPILLAR TRACKS ALLOW EXCAVATOR TO WORK ON UNEVEN GROUND

DIGGER BUCKET

Drainage

Water standing on a fast road is extremely dangerous. It may spray across windscreens so that drivers cannot see clearly, or may cause vehicles to skid. If water seeps through the road surface and then turns to ice, it expands and damages the layers of the road underneath. So before the carriageway is built, drainage pipes are laid to carry any water that penetrates the surface away to trenches at the side of the road.

Foundations

The best way to make a strong road surface is to build it in layers. The foundation of the carriageway is usually two layers of crushed stone, called **aggregate**. A 20 cm thick layer of large stones goes down first and is squashed flat by heavy rollers to pack the stones firmly together. A thinner, 8 cm layer of smaller pieces of aggregate follows. This is rolled again to make the foundations firm and to crush out any empty spaces.

Laying the pavement

Finally, the top layer, the pavement, is laid. This is the tough, waterproof surface on which traffic will travel. It must be smooth enough to give vehicles a comfortable ride, but not so smooth that their wheels cannot keep a grip on the road. (In road-building, the pavement is the road surface and not the pedestrian footpath.)

Paving and rolling

Road paving is a slow job. The paver moves along at less than 1 km/h spreading hot tarmac on to the road. The roller follows, flattening down the tarmac until the road surface is hard and smooth.

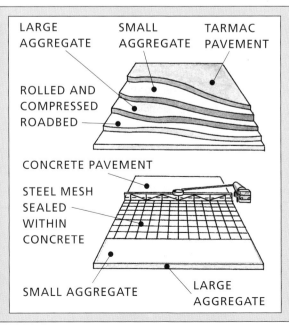

WORKERS RAKE ROAD SURFACE SMOOTH AND FLAT

METAL PLATE SPREADS TARMAC OVER ROAD SURFACE

ROAD-PAVER

ROAD-ROLLER

HOT TARMAC

The pavement is laid in one operation. The men rake away any bumps or holes before the road-roller (left) moves in.

Tarmac and concrete

Two types of material may be used for the pavement. One is tarmac or blacktop, a mix of tar and stone chips that hardens into an even surface. The other is concrete, a mixture of sand, gravel, water and cement. Concrete roads are laid in sections, with a strip of waterproof material between the concrete and the foundation.

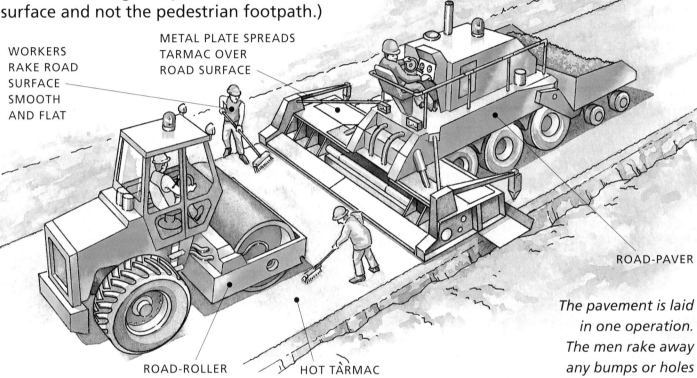

LARGE AGGREGATE

SMALL AGGREGATE

TARMAC PAVEMENT

ROLLED AND COMPRESSED ROADBED

CONCRETE PAVEMENT

STEEL MESH SEALED WITHIN CONCRETE

SMALL AGGREGATE

LARGE AGGREGATE

STEP BY STEP

4 The disc is loaded into a computer on a **drilling jumbo**. The jumbo then automatically drills holes in the correct places.

Finishing off

Once the road surface has hardened, a new army of workers moves in. Their job is to add the finishing touches which will make the road easy and safe to use.

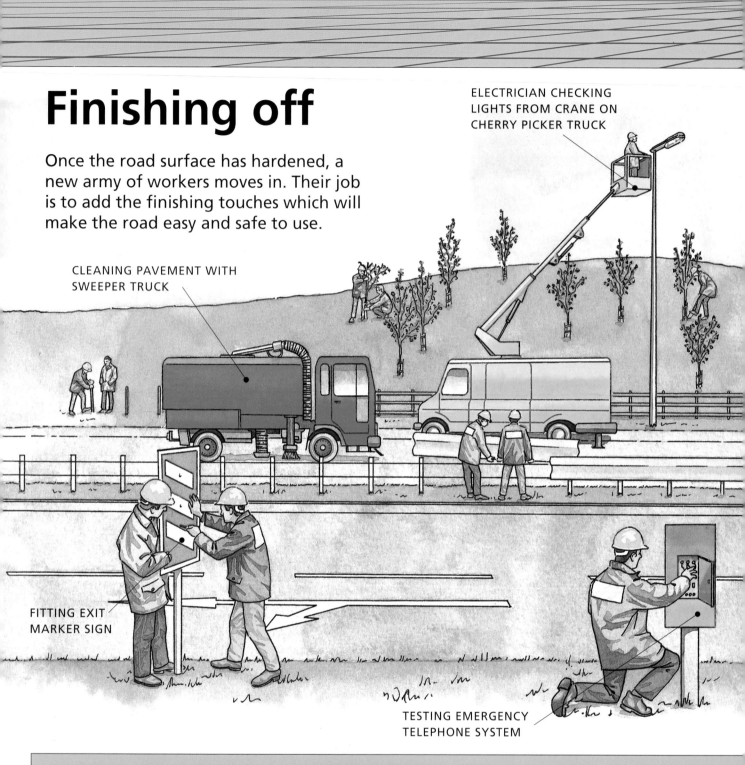

ELECTRICIAN CHECKING LIGHTS FROM CRANE ON CHERRY PICKER TRUCK

CLEANING PAVEMENT WITH SWEEPER TRUCK

FITTING EXIT MARKER SIGN

TESTING EMERGENCY TELEPHONE SYSTEM

Connecting up

Before the road can be used, lights and telephones must be installed. Many roads have lighting all the way along. Others have lights at **intersections**. Direction and warning signs must also be installed. All these lights and road signs are then fitted and connected up to the cables running under the road surface.

On the motorway

On motorways, emergency telephones fitted at the sides of the carriageways at intervals are connected to a central police control room. The control room also operates lighted signals by the side of the road. These warn drivers of bad weather conditions, and give information about road closures and temporary speed limits.

Safety measures

On a dual carriageway, steel crash barriers are built down the **central reservation** to prevent vehicles skidding from one carriageway onto the other. Steel supports are also put in position for road signs. These are carefully designed and positioned so that drivers can read them while travelling at high speeds. Cat's-eyes, which reflect the lights of approaching traffic, are embedded into the road pavement to mark the lanes and the edge of the carriageway. Arrows are painted on the surface to show drivers where to change lanes to enter or leave the road.

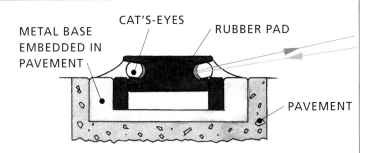

Above, cat's-eyes mark traffic lanes and exits.

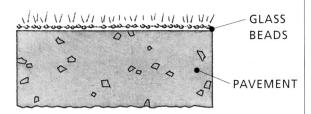

Above, tiny glass beads are mixed in with the paint used for road markings. They reflect the light from a driver's headlights.

White lane markings are laid by trucks which carry their own supply of quick-drying, hardwearing paint.

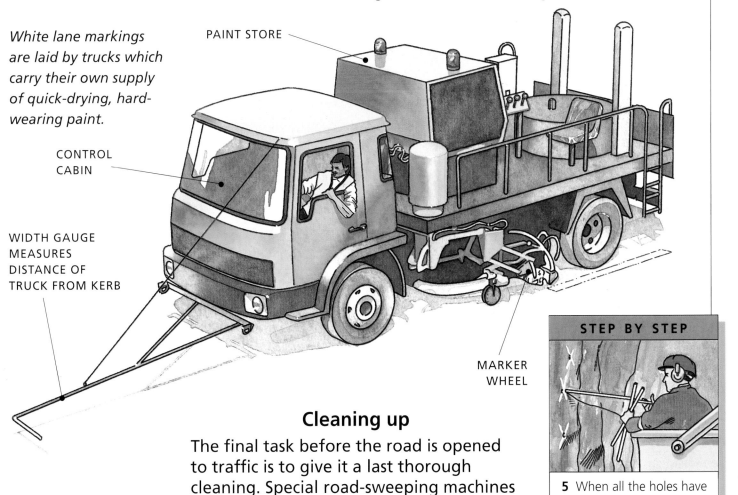

PAINT STORE

CONTROL CABIN

WIDTH GAUGE MEASURES DISTANCE OF TRUCK FROM KERB

MARKER WHEEL

Cleaning up

The final task before the road is opened to traffic is to give it a last thorough cleaning. Special road-sweeping machines remove dust, mud and any other debris left behind by the road builders.

STEP BY STEP

5 When all the holes have been made, they are filled with powerful explosives. The engineers know exactly how much explosive to use.

Flyovers and junctions

Major roads sometimes carry traffic over older city streets on **flyovers**. These overhead roadways keep long-distance traffic separate from traffic in the streets below and enable it to bypass city centres.

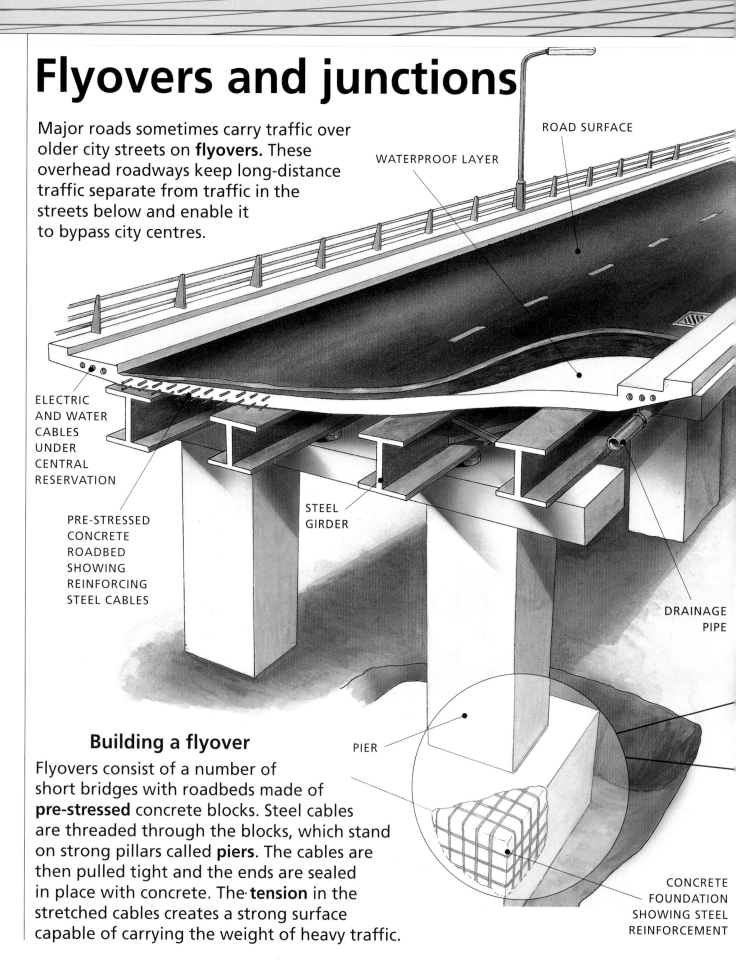

ROAD SURFACE

WATERPROOF LAYER

ELECTRIC AND WATER CABLES UNDER CENTRAL RESERVATION

PRE-STRESSED CONCRETE ROADBED SHOWING REINFORCING STEEL CABLES

STEEL GIRDER

DRAINAGE PIPE

PIER

CONCRETE FOUNDATION SHOWING STEEL REINFORCEMENT

Building a flyover

Flyovers consist of a number of short bridges with roadbeds made of **pre-stressed** concrete blocks. Steel cables are threaded through the blocks, which stand on strong pillars called **piers**. The cables are then pulled tight and the ends are sealed in place with concrete. The **tension** in the stretched cables creates a strong surface capable of carrying the weight of heavy traffic.

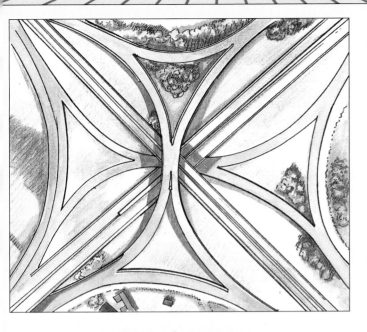

Interchanges

Where two major roads cross, traffic can transfer from one road to the other on a complicated layout called an **interchange.** One road is built above the other, and vehicles are carried between them on overpasses and underpasses which form the **junction**. Interchanges are built in different patterns. Some like the one above, take up a large area of land, so engineers try to think of designs which use less space.

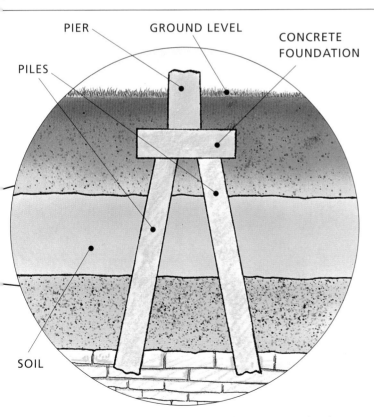

Cut-through section of a pier below ground. The pier is supported by concrete columns called **piles**.

Leaving and joining

On roads where traffic is travelling at high speeds, it is important that vehicles can join or leave the traffic smoothly and safely. At road junctions, short, sloped roads called **slip roads** allow vehicles joining a major road to merge gradually with the rest of the traffic. **Exit ramps** allow vehicles to leave the major road without crossing other lanes. The exit ramps usually lead to and from roundabouts which form a safe junction with the second road.

STEP BY STEP

6 An electric detonator is used to set the explosives off. The explosion removes slices of rock along the tunnel route.

The first roads

The first travellers on Earth were prehistoric hunter-gatherers, who moved from place to place in search of food. In about 10 000 BC, people began to live in settlements, but they still needed to travel around to trade goods. They chose the easiest routes, avoiding long climbs and difficult river crossings. These simple tracks were the world's first roads.

Imperial roads

The earliest empires grew up nearly 5000 years ago in the Middle East, China and South America. Their leaders ruled over vast areas of land. To stay in control, the leaders needed to move armies around quickly, so they used thousands of slaves to build roads. Traders soon found that military roads were faster and easier to use than the old tracks, so they began to travel along them, too.

*Thousands of years ago, Emperor Shih Huang Ti's troops marched down the huge network of roads he had built. When the emperor's tomb was rediscovered in the 1970s, magnificent **terracotta** copies of the soldiers were found.*

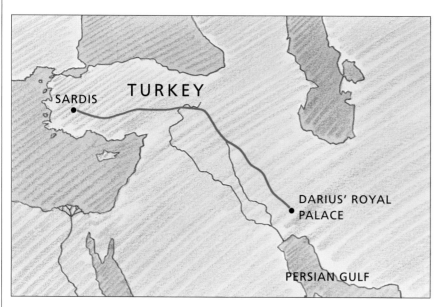

King Darius of Persia reigned from 521 to 486 BC. His great Royal Road ran 2700 km from Sardis in what is now Turkey to Darius' royal palace near the Persian Gulf.

Indian and Chinese roads

In about 270 BC, an Indian prince called Ashoka began to build up an empire across northern India. He was a peaceful ruler, but saw that good roads were essential for his empire to prosper. His roads were lined with trees to provide shade, and there were rest-houses where people could stay overnight. About 50 years later, in 221 BC, Shih Huang Ti became Emperor of China. He also built a vast network of roads along which his army could move to put down rebels or fight invaders.

Roman roads

The early Chinese and Indian roads disappeared a long time ago. But the roads of the Roman Empire, which lasted from about 27 BC to AD 476, were more skilfully built. Roman roads were planned by army engineers, who chose as straight a route as possible so that troops could march from place to place in the shortest possible time. Some stretches of Roman road can still be seen today.

Layer by layer

Roman builders began to construct a road by digging two trenches. Then they scraped away the loose earth between the trenches until the **sub-soil** was reached. In chalky areas, a layer of chalk was laid on the sub-soil and rammed into place to make a hard foundation. Where large stones were easily available, these were used instead. On top of this layer went a layer of flints or pebbles, with a scattering of chalk or limestone to fill the gaps between them. In towns, or on soft ground, the road surface was made of stone blocks. Elsewhere, local gravel was used for the top layer.

ROAD EDGING

CHALK
OR
LIMESTONE
BRUSHED IN
TO FILL GAPS

The Romans had no machinery to help with their road-building, but they had large work-forces of slaves, overseen by soldiers.

FOUNDATION OF LARGE STONES

LAYER
OF SMALLER
STONES

7 When all the dust and smoke has cleared, bulldozers pick up the rock fragments produced by the explosion.

New roads for new times

After the Roman Empire collapsed in about AD 476, Europe's road system fell apart. Mud, potholes and fallen rocks made travel hazardous. Few people travelled at night or in winter.

Road revival

In the eighteenth century, the growth of industry and trade in Europe made better roads essential. France was the first country to plan a national road system, followed by Spain, parts of Germany, and Britain. Britain's two great road builders were Thomas Telford and John McAdam, both Scotsmen. In the first thirty years of the nineteenth century, they created a road system which was ideal for fast, horse-drawn traffic.

A European street scene in the sixteenth century. Even in the cities the roads were littered with rocks and rubbish.

In the Middle Ages, roads were little more than muddy tracks, making travel difficult and often dangerous.

Following the Romans

The old Roman roads were the basis of Telford and McAdam's network. They both realized, like the Romans, that good drainage was very important. So they dug down to the foundations of the Roman roads, re-surveyed and levelled the roadbeds, and then built up new carriageways. McAdam's method was to place large stones on the roadbed, followed by a layer of smaller ones. The top layer consisted of even smaller stones or gravel. His roads were cambered, with gutters to carry away rainwater.

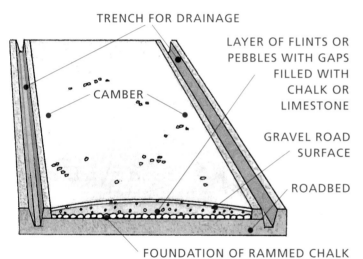

TRENCH FOR DRAINAGE

LAYER OF FLINTS OR PEBBLES WITH GAPS FILLED WITH CHALK OR LIMESTONE

CAMBER

GRAVEL ROAD SURFACE

ROADBED

FOUNDATION OF RAMMED CHALK

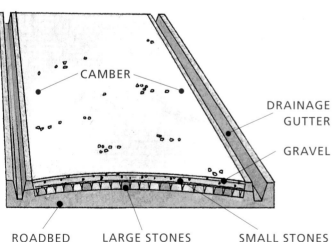

CAMBER

DRAINAGE GUTTER

GRAVEL

ROADBED   LARGE STONES   SMALL STONES

Above top, a typical Roman road. Below, the Roman method adapted by John McAdam, with a less steep camber than the Romans used.

Britain's first motorway under construction in 1959. Britain was the last major industrialized country to build a motorway network.

High-speed roads

The development of petrol- and diesel-engined vehicles in the late nineteenth century led to a need for even better roads. At first, the answer was to make the existing roads more hard-wearing and less dusty by adding a tarmac surface. But as traffic increased it became clear that new roads, specially designed for heavy, high-speed traffic, were needed. In the 1920s and 1930s, the USA began to build its national highways, Germany its Autobahns, France its autoroutes and Italy its autostrada. Britain improved its existing roads, but did not open its first motorway, between London and Birmingham, until 1959.

STEP BY STEP

8 The waste material, called **muck** or **spoil**, is loaded into large dumper trucks and carried out of the new tunnel.

19

Roads in North America

Early settlers in North America used the sea, rivers, and local tracks for the small amount of travel they did. But as early as 1780, President George Washington saw the need for a network of roads into the interior of the USA.

The Santa Fe Trail

In 1802, work started on the USA's first major road, which ran from Independence, Missouri, to the trading post at Santa Fe, which was then in Mexico. The opening of the road encouraged the establishment of profitable trade links between Mexico and the USA. The road is now known as the Santa Fe Trail or sometimes the National Old Trails Road.

The National Road

In 1811, work began on the National Road which was the first **federal** highway in the USA. At first it ran only a short way, from Cumberland, Maryland, to Wheeling, West Virginia. Later, in 1838, it was extended eastwards to Vandalia, Illinois. Travellers on the road had to pay a toll (fee).

The Oregon Trail

In the 1840s, large numbers of Americans travelled west to open up the rich Oregon farmland. They founded the Oregon Trail, which ran for 3200 km from Independence, Missouri to Portland, Oregon. The trail was a simple track along which guides led the wagon trains.

A wagon train takes pioneer settlers, travelling together for safety with an experienced guide, into the far west of the USA.

The first superhighway

The invention of the motor car in the late nineteenth century led to the paving of sections of roads in the USA, but it was not until the 1920s that the government began a nationwide scheme of road improvements. In 1940, the first American 'superhighway' was opened between Harrisburg and Pittsburgh in Pennsylvania, a distance of 256 km. This was the first road to have restaurants and filling stations at regular intervals along it.

The Blue Mountain tunnel on the Pennsylvania Turnpike.

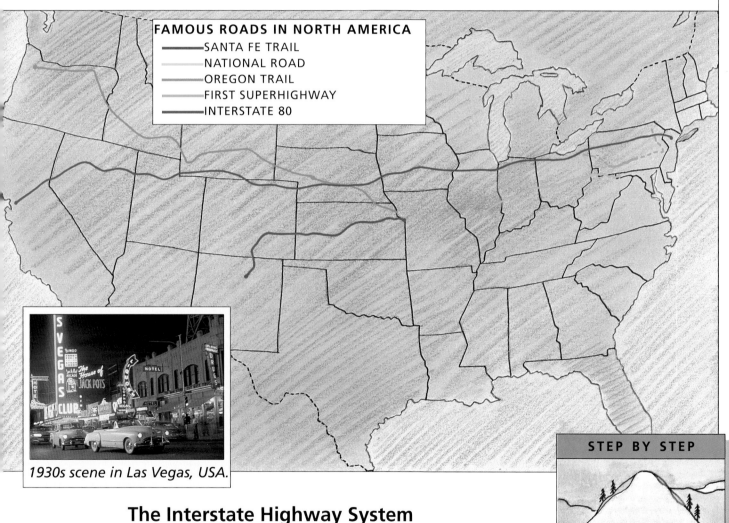

FAMOUS ROADS IN NORTH AMERICA
——————— SANTA FE TRAIL
——————— NATIONAL ROAD
——————— OREGON TRAIL
——————— FIRST SUPERHIGHWAY
——————— INTERSTATE 80

1930s scene in Las Vegas, USA.

STEP BY STEP

9 This process is repeated many times to build a complete tunnel. To save time, long tunnels are often built from both ends.

The Interstate Highway System

Another programme of improvements began in 1956 with the start of the Interstate Highway System, of which Interstate 80 is one example. The system was designed to link most cities with a population of over 50 000. When complete, the Interstate network will consist of nearly 69 000 km of high-speed, multiple-lane roads covering the country.

Famous roads and routes

Many roads are built, used and later forgotten when they fall into disrepair. But, for a variety of reasons, a few roads become famous.

Marco Polo, the first European to explore China, travelled the Silk Road in the thirteenth century.

The Silk Road

It is over 2000 years since traders and their **caravans** of camels began to carry goods along the Silk Road. This ancient trade route ran for over 6400 km, linking China in the East with Europe in the West. Today, half the route is a paved highway. In other places it is just a track.

East meets West

The Silk Road crosses some of the most dangerous **terrain** on Earth. Starting from Xi'an in China, the road crosses the Taklamakan Desert, the Pamir Mountains north of India, and the rocky wastes of Afghanistan and Iran before reaching the Mediterranean Sea near Antioch in Turkey.

The Appian Way

The Appian Way, running southwards from Rome, Italy, was the most famous Roman road. Its construction began in 312 BC. At first, the road ran only as far as Capua, 212 km from Rome, but later it was extended for another 376 km to Brindisi, a port much further south. Thousands of slaves working for military engineers built the road, which was paved with stone. The work involved draining the Pontine Marshes, south of Rome, and building bridges and embankments. Parts of the Appian Way remained in use until the twentieth century, and the modern road mainly follows the same route.

A camel train on the Silk Road.

The Great North Road

The Great North Road forms the spine of Britain's road system. It runs for 630 km between London and Edinburgh, Scotland. The southern end of the road was built by the Romans and linked London with Hadrian's Wall, which the Romans built across the north of England.

Military use

Like all Roman roads, the Great North Road was designed for military use. After AD 410, when the Romans left Britain, the road was neglected. From 1600, patchy repairs were made, and stage coaches began to use the road. The modern A1 follows the route of the old Roman road.

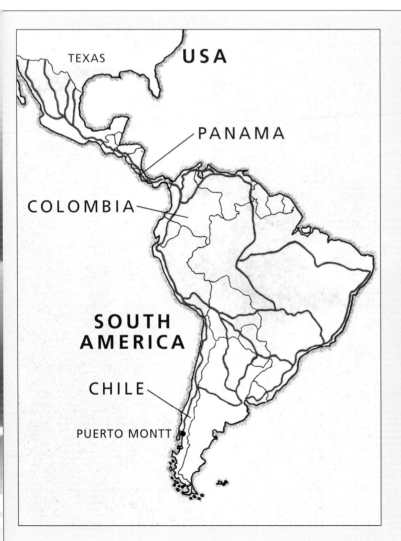

The Pan-American Highway

In 1923, the governments of North and South America began to plan the building of a Pan-American Highway which would run from Texas, USA, to Puerto Montt in Chile. Work began in 1936 and lasted for 50 years. The road runs through tropical jungle and across mountain passes as well as through the dry deserts of the mid-western USA. The 400 km section of highway that runs through the densely forested border between Panama and Colombia is still to be completed.

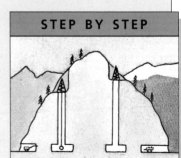

STEP BY STEP

10 Shafts are sometimes drilled down to the tunnel so that work can carry on in several places at the same time.

Tunnels

Tunnels take roads and railways under obstructions such as water, mountains or buildings. They may also carry **sewage**, water and pipelines for gas or oil. Railways run in tunnels beneath many of the world's major cities. Taking roads and railways through tunnels avoids long diversions and cuts journey times. Sometimes a tunnel is the only way of making a journey by land – for example, crossing the Alps between Switzerland and Italy. Tunnels are so expensive to build that they are used only if there is no alternative.

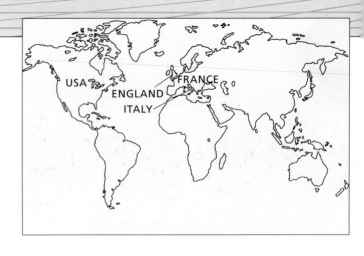

Construction methods

Large tunnels can be built in three main ways. The usual method today is to bore a hole underground or underwater, using explosives or tunnel-boring machines. Another method of building underwater is to lower a sunken tube tunnel from barges moored on the surface. The third method is called **cut-and-cover**. Builders cut a deep trench underground, build the tunnel inside it and cover the surface again. Cut-and-cover tunnels can only be built if there are no buildings in the way.

Metropolitan Railway Factfile ▼

Location:	London, England
Type:	Cut-and-cover rail tunnel
From:	Farringdon Street
To:	Paddington
Length:	6.5 km
Built:	Early 1860s

The Farringdon Street to Paddington section of the Metropolitan Railway was the world's first underground railway. It opened for traffic in 1863, with trains hauled by steam locomotives.

Mont Cenis Tunnel Factfile ▶

Location: Southern France/northern Italy
Type: Mountain rail tunnel
From: Savoy Province, France
To: Turin Province, Italy
Length: 14 km
Built: 1857-1871

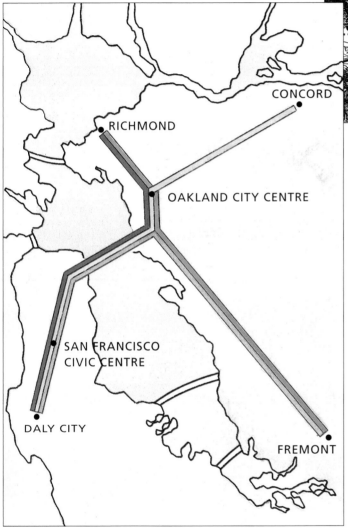

CONCORD

RICHMOND

OAKLAND CITY CENTRE

SAN FRANCISCO
CIVIC CENTRE

DALY CITY

FREMONT

Mont Cenis rail tunnel links France to Italy through the Alps, beneath Frejus Peak. When building began in 1857, engineers expected to progress at only 22 cm a day for 20 years.

◀ BART Tunnel Factfile

Location: San Francisco, California
Type: Sunken tube rail tunnel
Length: 5.8 km
Built: 1960s

BART stands for Bay Area Rapid Transit. This is a system of underground and overland railways covering the area around San Francisco, USA. The BART tunnel is the longest underwater passenger tunnel in the USA.

Fitting out

Building the tunnel is only the first stage of making a new transport link. When engineers have checked the tunnel to make sure that it is safe, other experts move in. Railway tracks or road carriageways are laid through the tunnel. Exits and entrances are built. The tunnel's lighting, communications systems and signals are installed. Road or rail traffic makes test runs to make sure that everything works perfectly, and only then is the tunnel opened.

STEP BY STEP

11 Engineers use laser beams to check that the work is on course and that the two tunnels will meet in the middle.

Investigating the route

The cost of a tunnel is uppermost in engineers' minds at the planning stage. All tunnels are expensive to build, but problems which occur in the course of building may send the cost up even higher.

Surveying the ground

Because of the high costs, the first stage in planning an underground or underwater tunnel is to make a **geological survey** of the route. Geologists drill boreholes using a hollow drill. This takes out cores or samples of the soil and rocks beneath. These cores give a picture of the ground through which the tunnel will be built and show up soft mud, underground lakes, or any other obstacles which the route should avoid. The cores also help engineers to decide what equipment will be needed for tunnelling, how many workers will have to be employed, how much the work is likely to cost and how long it will take.

Geologists using a mobile drilling rig to drill test bores.

DRILLING RIG

DRILL STRING LOWERS PIPES INTO GROUND

WHEELS TRANSPORT RIG FROM THE SITE

DRILL PIPES

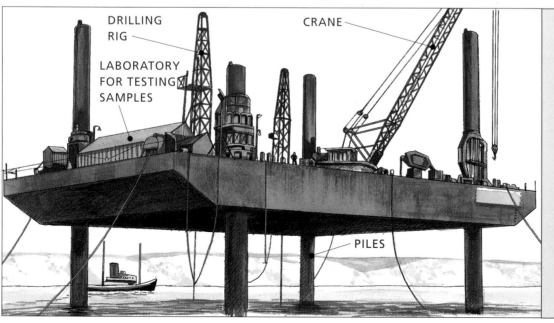

DRILLING RIG

LABORATORY FOR TESTING SAMPLES

CRANE

PILES

Drilling from a platform in the English Channel for core samples of rock during the route planning of the Channel Tunnel. Rock samples were drilled from depths up to 80m below the sea-bed.

Flood danger

Drainage is important in all tunnels. There is always a danger of flooding, even in tunnels under the ground. Water trapped in soil, sand or gravel or from streams and lakes below ground often collects in the tunnel. Workers and equipment must be protected from flood water while the tunnel is being built, and an efficient pumping and drainage system must also be part of the completed tunnel.

A pumping station at the Dartford Tunnel near London, England. Instruments keep a check on water seepage in the tunnel and the pumps can be brought into action instantly.

Connecting links

Building a tunnel usually means that the road or rail connections at each end must be improved. The money needed for these is part of the cost of the whole project. New railway junctions and stations, motorway **spur roads** and parking areas, signal boxes and control rooms may all be necessary. These must be planned and sited at the same time as the tunnel route is decided.

At work on the approach to a new tunnel in London's developing Docklands area. Approach roads are often built first to give easy access to tunnel sites.

STEP BY STEP

12 The new tunnel is lined with steel mesh to keep small pieces of rock from falling and to strengthen the tunnel walls.

Tunnelling under water

Tunnels built under water are among the greatest achievements of modern engineering because their construction presents special problems. The sea- or river-bed along which an underwater tunnel runs, contains soft sand, mud and other **sediments** which must be kept out of the workings. Water seeping through from above is another hazard. The tunnel entrances, called portals, are sited some distance away from the water so that there is a gradual slope down to the underwater level.

Boring through the ground

Soft ground under water is fairly easy to drill through using tunnel-boring machines. Special cutting heads are added to excavate rock. The huge boring machines cut away at the surface in front of them and carry the waste material, called spoil or muck, away on conveyor belts. Trucks then take it to the mouth of the tunnel. The cutting heads are pushed forwards by fluid-powered **hydraulic jacks**. Workers behind the cutting heads are protected by a metal shield which is filled with compressed air to stop any leakage of water into the tunnel. Newly bored tunnels are lined with steel and concrete.

CUTTING HEAD

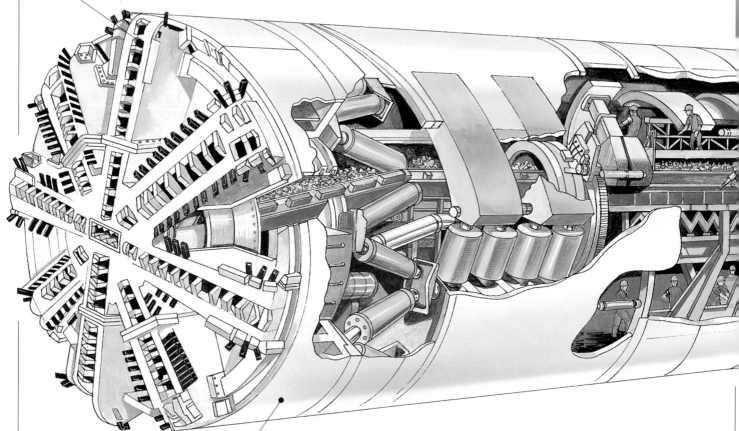

METAL SHIELD

To save time, tunnels are often built by two teams of workers starting from opposite ends. Careful calculations are essential to make sure that the two tunnels will meet accurately in the middle.

Side by side

If the new tunnel is designed to carry large amounts of traffic, two tunnels are usually built side by side, one for each direction of travel. Two narrow tunnels resist the pressures above them better than one larger one. Often a third tunnel, the service tunnel, is added for use by maintenance workers, who carry out any necessary repairs, and by emergency services.

Sunken tube tunnels

Underwater tunnels can also be built using steel tubes. These sunken tube tunnels are suitable only for quite short distances. They consist of sections of steel tube, each up to 100m long, which are made in factories and sealed at each end. While the tubes are being made, special boats called dredgers cut a deep trench on the sea- or river-bed.

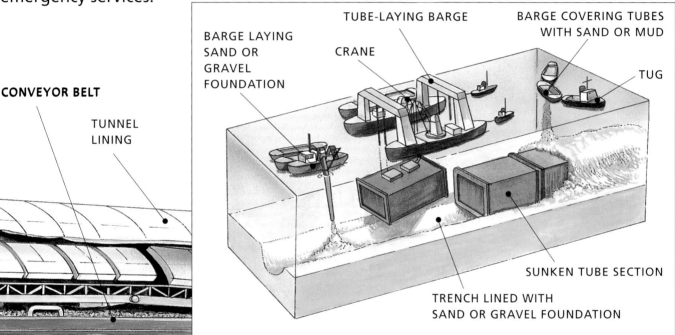

BARGE LAYING SAND OR GRAVEL FOUNDATION

TUBE-LAYING BARGE

CRANE

BARGE COVERING TUBES WITH SAND OR MUD

TUG

CONVEYOR BELT

TUNNEL LINING

SUNKEN TUBE SECTION

TRENCH LINED WITH SAND OR GRAVEL FOUNDATION

Calm weather conditions are critical for the laying of a sunken tube tunnel, a complex operation in which many separate stages must be brought together in sequence.

Completing the tunnel

To complete a sunken tube tunnel, the tubes are floated out on barges and lowered into place. Divers bolt the sections together, and the joints are sealed with concrete. The tunnel is covered with sand and mud to protect it from damage. Finally, the seals at the ends of each tube are cut away and the tubes are **welded** together.

13 Next the mesh is sprayed with layers of liquid concrete called **shotcrete.** This prevents water seeping into the tunnel.

The Channel Tunnel

The Channel Tunnel carries rail passengers and vehicles under the English Channel between England and France – a distance of almost 50 km. There are two main tunnels, each 7.3m in diameter, with a service tunnel between them. On average, the tunnel runs 45m below the sea-bed, but in some places it is 75m under the ground. The tunnel entrances, called portals, are sited some distance from the water so that there is a gradual slope down to the underwater level. The British terminal, just outside Folkestone in Kent, and the French terminal at Calais are each nearly 10 km from the coast.

French and British tunnellers shaking hands as they meet in the middle of the Channel Tunnel.

False starts

Building the Channel Tunnel was the biggest European engineering project in history. A tunnel was first suggested by the French Emperor Napoleon in 1802. Many engineers produced plans in the nineteenth century, and in the 1880s a start was made to the tunnel on both sides of the Channel. But two world wars revived British fears of invasion from Europe, and it was not until the 1960s that the idea of the Channel Tunnel came up again.

Meeting in the middle

The building of the tunnel finally began in 1987 and was completed in 1994. It involved removing 8 million cubic metres of spoil and lining the tunnel with 1.8 million tonnes of steel and concrete. British and French tunnellers worked from each end, building the service tunnel first. When they met they found that they had been working accurately to within a few centimetres.

A section through the Channel Tunnel. Each main tunnel carries trains in one direction only. The smaller service tunnel is used for maintenance. Cross passages link all three tunnels at intervals. The smaller arched link is an air duct.

POWER CABLE CARRYING ELECTRICITY TO TRAIN MOTORS

MAIN TUNNEL

Cars by rail

It was decided at the start that the Channel Tunnel would carry rail traffic only, using electric trains. This avoided what would have been the enormous problem of ventilating a 50-km tunnel filled with exhaust fumes. Cars and trucks are loaded on to specially designed wagons for the 35-minute journey. Motorists and truck drivers can travel by road as far as the terminals on each side and board trains for the underwater journey. Alternatively, passengers without vehicles may join high speed trains in Paris, Brussels or London and travel straight through without stopping.

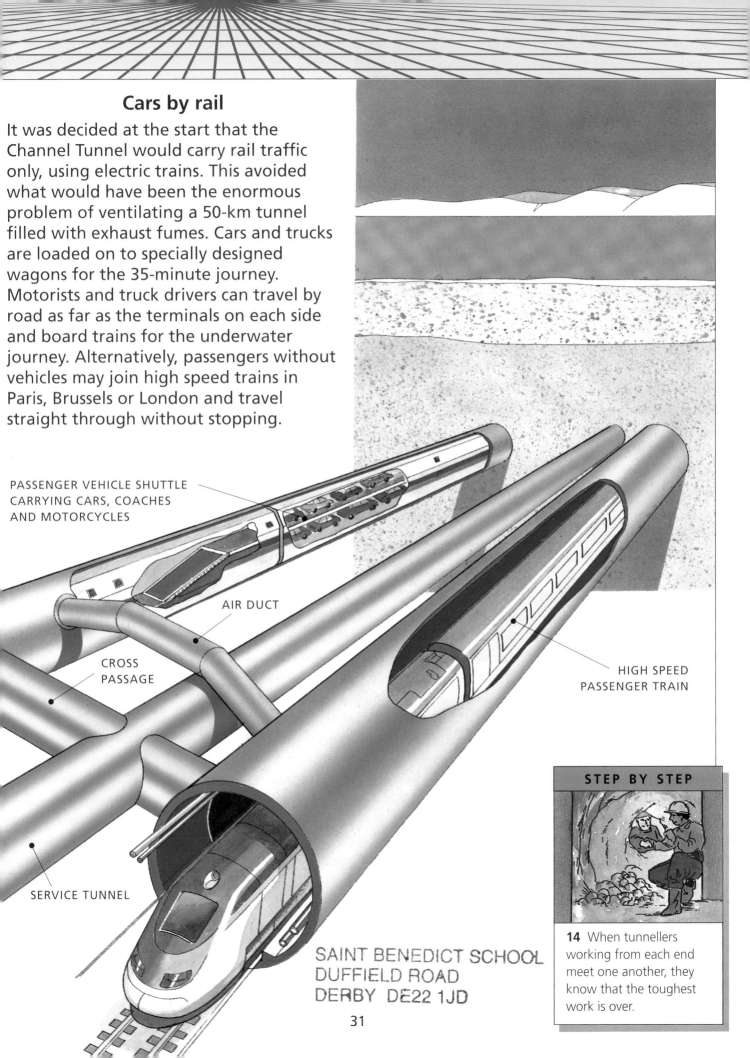

PASSENGER VEHICLE SHUTTLE CARRYING CARS, COACHES AND MOTORCYCLES

AIR DUCT

CROSS PASSAGE

HIGH SPEED PASSENGER TRAIN

SERVICE TUNNEL

SAINT BENEDICT SCHOOL
DUFFIELD ROAD
DERBY DE22 1JD

STEP BY STEP

14 When tunnellers working from each end meet one another, they know that the toughest work is over.

Tunnelling through mountains

Tunnel-boring machines are not powerful enough to bore through the hard rock that is often found in mountainous areas. Engineers building tunnels beneath mountains usually have to use explosives to blast their way through. This is a very exact science. Engineers know exactly where and how to drill the holes to be packed with explosive, and how much explosive to use.

Drilling jumbos

The usual method is to drill a large number of holes, each packed with a carefully calculated amount of explosive. Workers use a machine called a jumbo which can drill many holes at the same time. When everyone has retreated to a safe distance, the explosives are set off by an electric spark from a detonator.

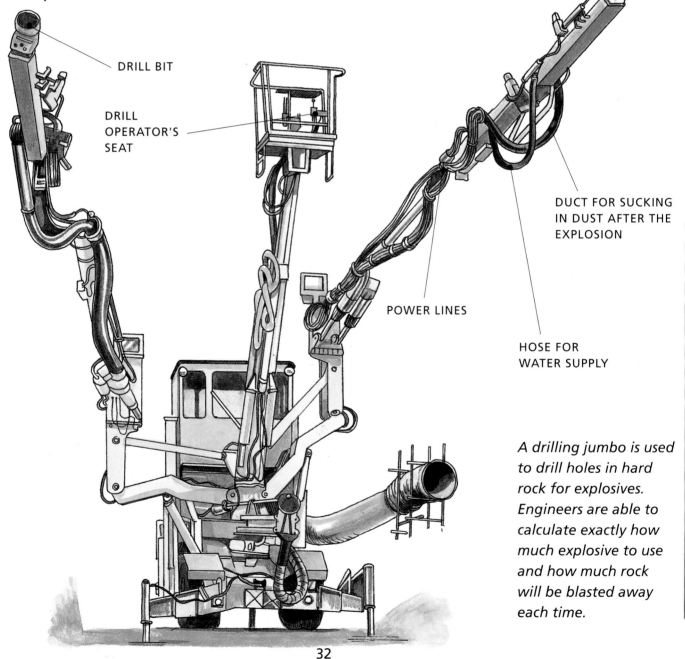

DRILL BIT

DRILL OPERATOR'S SEAT

DUCT FOR SUCKING IN DUST AFTER THE EXPLOSION

POWER LINES

HOSE FOR WATER SUPPLY

A drilling jumbo is used to drill holes in hard rock for explosives. Engineers are able to calculate exactly how much explosive to use and how much rock will be blasted away each time.

After the blast

When the smoke and dust have cleared, large excavators, called front-end loaders, move in to clear away the broken rock and rubble, while the jumbo moves ahead to tackle the next section of rock face. Behind the front-end loaders come the roof-lining teams. Sometimes lining is not necessary, but mountain tunnels are usually given a lining of steel mesh to keep small pieces of rock from falling, or one of concrete to prevent the seepage of water.

Wires are run from the explosive charges to a safe distance where the explosives will be detonated by an electric spark.

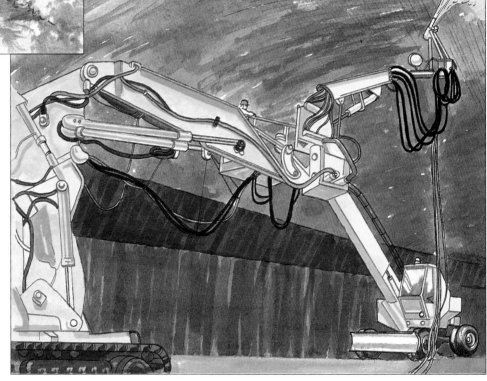

One method of lining a tunnel is to use sheets of steel mesh which are welded together.

Hot and cold

One of the problems of tunnelling through mountains is the wide range of temperatures that workers have to face deep underground. During the building of the Simplon Tunnel between Switzerland and Italy, which started in 1906, workers could only carry on if the rocks were sprayed continuously with cold water. When the Mont Blanc Tunnel between France and Italy was built in the 1960s, the temperature fell to -14^0 C.

STEP BY STEP

15 Once a road tunnel has been completed and lined, road-building can begin. The roadbed goes down first.

Early tunnels

Tunnels have been built throughout history for many different reasons. The Ancient Egyptians tunnelled into the rocks of Nubia, on the Upper Nile, to mine gold. In the twelfth century BC, the **Etruscans** hollowed out tunnels as burial places for their dead. But the greatest tunnellers were the Ancient Romans.

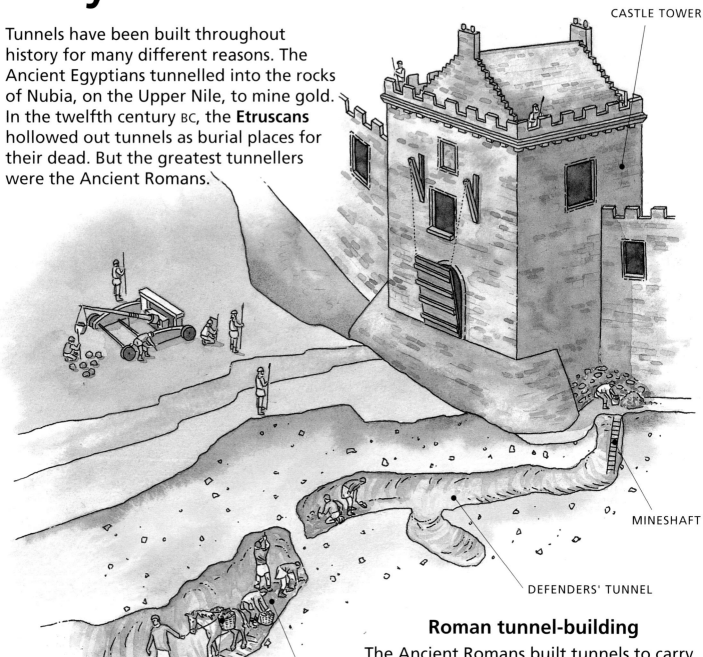

CASTLE TOWER

MINESHAFT

DEFENDERS' TUNNEL

ATTACKERS' TUNNEL

RUBBLE TAKEN AWAY BY PACKHORSE

Both the attackers and defenders of St Andrew's Castle in Scotland dug tunnels during a siege in the winter of 1546-47. The defenders managed to find their enemies' tunnel and stopped the advance.

Roman tunnel-building

The Ancient Romans built tunnels to carry water and sewage beneath the streets of their cities. They first perfected a way of tunnelling by lighting fires in the rock. When the rock was red hot, they threw cold water on it. This caused the rock to break up, and the debris was then cleared away, making a section of tunnel. The operation was repeated until the tunnel was finished.

Tunnels in wartime

Tunnels were often used in war. In the **Middle Ages**, soldiers dug tunnels under the walls of enemy cities, using timber to prop up the walls and roofs. Soldiers also dug tunnels under enemy lines in the **trench warfare** in northern France and Belgium during the course of the First World War (1914-1918).

Tunnels for mines

By the fifteenth century, a growing shortage of wood for fuel led to the search for underground coal. The first coal mines were dug in the sides of hills. They were called **drift** mines, and led to the coalface through a horizontal tunnel. In later mines, tunnels were dug in the coal from **shafts** sunk in the ground. This meant that coal could be mined from **seams** way below the surface.

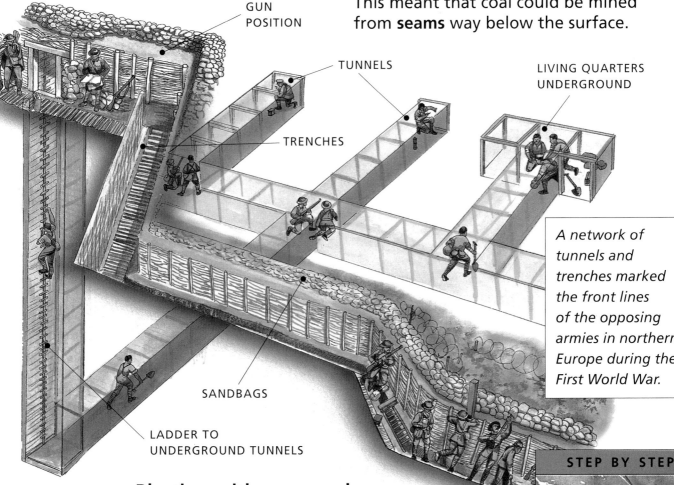

GUN POSITION

TUNNELS

TRENCHES

LIVING QUARTERS UNDERGROUND

SANDBAGS

LADDER TO UNDERGROUND TUNNELS

A network of tunnels and trenches marked the front lines of the opposing armies in northern Europe during the First World War.

Blasting with gunpowder

The first explosive used for tunnel-building was gunpowder. This was rammed into holes drilled in the rock. When the gunpowder exploded, it shattered the rock into small pieces which could then be cleared away. Gunpowder was first used in this way in 1660 to build a canal tunnel in France, and in the nineteenth century it was used to blast many of the first railway tunnels through rock. But gunpowder was dangerous to use, and the fumes after the explosions made working conditions unpleasant.

STEP BY STEP

16 Road-laying machines lay the road surface. The road-paver spreads the tarmac and the road-roller flattens down the surface.

New methods

In 1867, a Swedish scientist, Alfred Nobel, invented a new explosive which he called dynamite. This was more powerful than gunpowder and safer to use because its explosion could be calculated scientifically. The old method of setting off explosives was to lay a fuse between the engineer and the explosive. But this method was unreliable and there were many accidents. In the late nineteenth century, the fuse was replaced by electric wire connected to a detonator. This was safer, because engineers knew that as soon as the current was switched on the explosive would detonate.

Brunel's shield

Explosives cannot be used to build tunnels in soft ground or under water. In 1818, a French engineer who had settled in Britain, Marc Isambard Brunel, invented the first tunnelling shield, made of cast iron and timber. This huge cylinder protected 36 men digging inside it, and was pushed forward as work progressed. Workers followed behind to line the tunnel with brick.

MEN WORKING INSIDE SHIELD

CAST-IRON TUNNEL LINING

MUCK WAGON

Brunel's shield seen from behind. The cast-iron tunnel lining is being bolted in place. The muck, or waste material, is taken away to the end of the tunnel.

A cross-section of Brunel's tunnel under the River Thames. The tunnel, which took 15 years to complete, stretched from Wapping, on the north bank, to Rotherhithe, on the south bank.

The first underwater tunnel

Brunel used his shield to build the world's first underwater tunnel beneath the River Thames in London in 1824. The tunnel was 406m long. At first, it was a pedestrian tunnel, but it is now used by underground trains. Brunel's shield was a great breakthrough in tunnel-building. There was now no challenge that the engineers could not meet.

Brunel organized a banquet inside the tunnel to thank his workforce, and to prove to the public that the tunnel was perfectly safe to use.

STEP BY STEP

17 Teams of workers move in to instal emergency telephones, lights and air-conditioning. Cat's-eyes are embedded into the road.

Famous tunnels

Some tunnels have become famous, often because of their length or the skill used to build them. The Channel Tunnel is one example, but there are many more.

The Seikan Tunnel

The Seikan Tunnel carries railway trains between the Japanese islands of Hokkaido and Honshu, beneath the Strait of Tsugaru. The tunnel is almost 54 km long. Over 23 km of its length is under water, reaching a depth of 240m below sea level. Engineers started work on the tunnel in 1946, but it was not finished and brought into service until 1988.

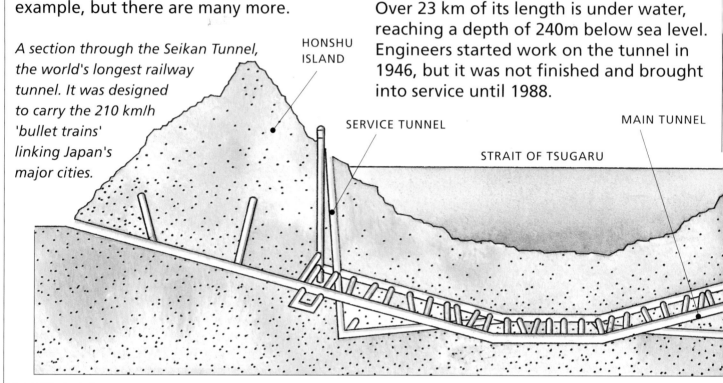

A section through the Seikan Tunnel, the world's longest railway tunnel. It was designed to carry the 210 km/h 'bullet trains' linking Japan's major cities.

HONSHU ISLAND

SERVICE TUNNEL

MAIN TUNNEL

STRAIT OF TSUGARU

The Chesapeake Tunnel Bridge

The Chesapeake Tunnel Bridge is a crossing of Chesapeake Bay on the Atlantic coast of the USA. It combines bridges, artificial islands and two sunken tube tunnels. This design was chosen so that large ocean-going ships could pass into the bay without difficulty. Each sunken tube tunnel is 3 km long and entered through portals on the artificial islands. These are in turn linked by bridges to the shores of the bay. Work on the scheme began in 1958 and the whole 28 km-long crossing opened in 1964.

One of the artificial islands which form part of the Chesapeake Tunnel Bridge. Beyond the island is the approach to a sunken tube tunnel section.

The St Gotthard Pass Tunnels

Two tunnels carry road and rail traffic beneath the St Gotthard Pass in the Swiss Alps. The rail tunnel, built between 1872 and 1882, climbs to a height of 1154m. In 1980, the St Gotthard Road Tunnel was opened. At a length of 16.4 km, this is the longest road tunnel in the world.

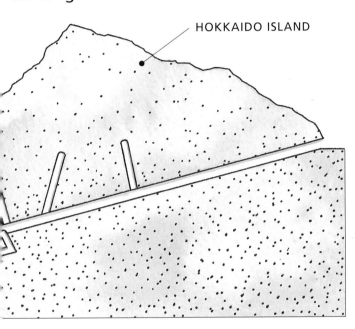

HOKKAIDO ISLAND

The St Gotthard Road Tunnel in Switzerland lies above the old road, which crossed the pass in a series of terrifying hairpin bends.

The Mont Blanc Road Tunnel

The Mont Blanc Road Tunnel carries vehicles from France to Italy beneath Europe's highest mountain. In 1959, teams of engineers began blasting the route from each side. They met, almost exactly on course, three years later. The tunnel was opened to traffic in 1965. The Mont Blanc Tunnel is 11.25 km long and passes about 3500m below the mountain peak.

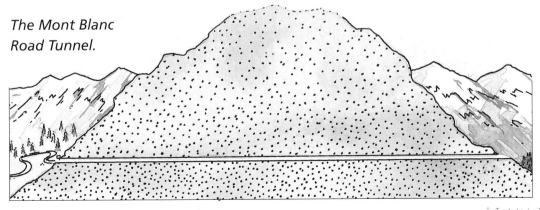

The Mont Blanc Road Tunnel.

STEP BY STEP

18 Before the road tunnel can be opened, it is checked thoroughly by engineers to make sure it is safe to use.

Road and tunnel facts

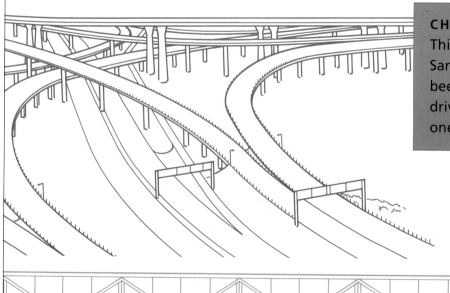

CHANGING DIRECTION
This complicated interchange at San Diego, California, USA, has been carefully designed so that drivers can safely change from one road to another.

PAY AS YOU ENTER
The idea of making people pay to use roads began in England in 1663, when gates were set up on parts of the Great North Road and road-users had to pay to be allowed through. The system was soon adopted all over the country. Today, in many countries, drivers have to pay tolls to use certain roads, bridges and tunnels. The money is used to pay for repairs. These tollgates are on a French autoroute.

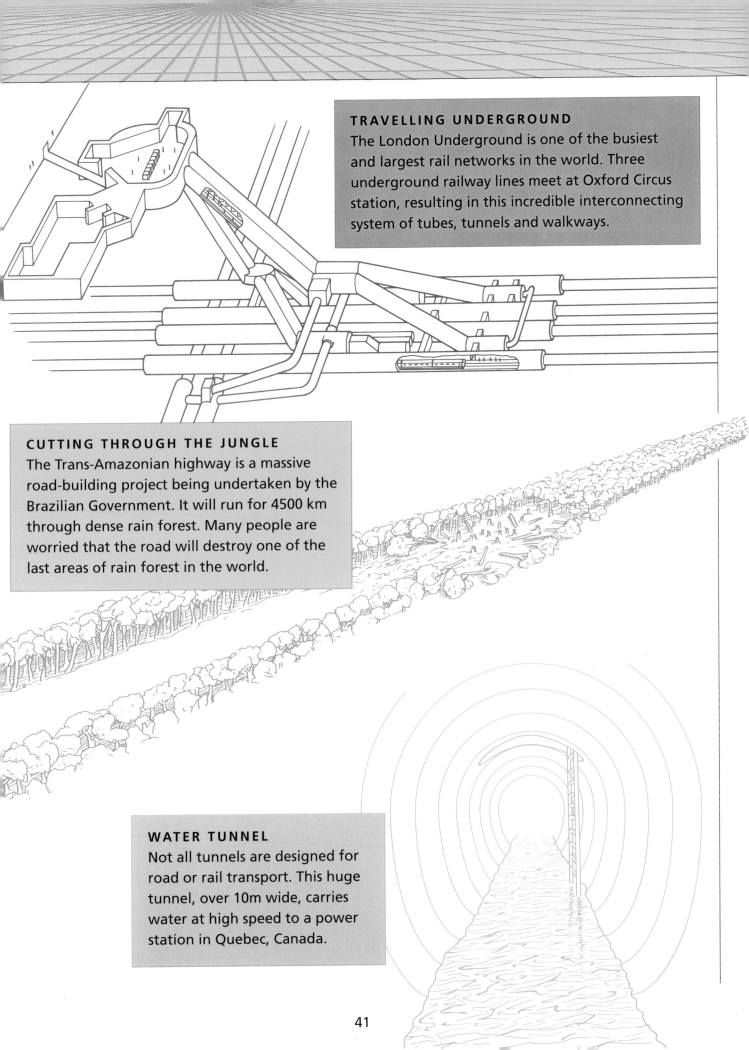

TRAVELLING UNDERGROUND
The London Underground is one of the busiest and largest rail networks in the world. Three underground railway lines meet at Oxford Circus station, resulting in this incredible interconnecting system of tubes, tunnels and walkways.

CUTTING THROUGH THE JUNGLE
The Trans-Amazonian highway is a massive road-building project being undertaken by the Brazilian Government. It will run for 4500 km through dense rain forest. Many people are worried that the road will destroy one of the last areas of rain forest in the world.

WATER TUNNEL
Not all tunnels are designed for road or rail transport. This huge tunnel, over 10m wide, carries water at high speed to a power station in Quebec, Canada.

Time chart

See how roads and tunnels have developed over the centuries with this time chart, which shows key roads and tunnels and when they were built.

c stands for circa, which means about. It is used before ancient dates that may not be accurate.

C 500 BC
Darius, King of Persia, builds the 2700 km 'Royal Road' across his empire.

312
The Roman general Claudius begins building the Appian Way from Rome to Capua.

272
Ashoka becomes king of the Mauryan Empire in northern India and begins to build a road system across it.

C 230
Shih Huang Ti, Emperor of China, begins building a network of roads across China, including one which runs along the top of the Great Wall.

C 100
The Silk Road is in use between China and the West.

36
Romans build the first road tunnel in Naples.

FIRST CENTURY AD

43
Roman road-building begins in Britain. An 8000 km network is planned, and building goes on until AD 81.

476
The Roman Empire collapses, and roads in Europe gradually fall into a state of disrepair.

C 1500
High point of the Inca Empire in South America. A network of roads links the empire's cities and villages.

1660
In France, gunpowder is used to build a tunnel.

1663
Tollgates are introduced on parts of the Great North Road in England.

1706
The first of over 1000 turnpike trusts, allowing road tolls to be collected in England, is created by Parliament.

1750
The London to Edinburgh stage coach takes 10 days to make the 630 km journey.

1756
John McAdam, Scottish roadbuilder, is born.

1757
Thomas Telford, Scottish roadbuilder and engineer, is born.

1780
George Washington orders the planning of the USA's first national road, from Washington DC to Santa Fe.

1795
Toll roads are introduced in the USA.

1818
Marc Isambard Brunel invents the tunnelling shield.

1824
Marc Isambard Brunel begins work on the world's first underwater tunnel beneath the River Thames in London.

1830
The London to Edinburgh stagecoach takes only two days to complete its journey.

C 1840s
Railways, with their faster journey times, cause the decline of coach services throughout Europe. This leads to the neglect of the road system. The pattern is repeated in the USA twenty years later.

1867
Alfred Nobel invents dynamite.

1872
Work begins on the St Gotthard Rail Tunnel in the Swiss Alps.

1887
Alfred Nobel invents **gelignite**.

1906
Work begins on the first Simplon Rail Tunnel between Switzerland and Italy.

1921
The US government plans a network of interstate highways.

1923
Planning of the Pan-American Highway begins.

1924
Construction begins on Italy's first autostrada (high-speed motorway).

1930
Germany's first Autobahn (motorway) opens.

1936
Work begins on the Pan-American Highway.

1946
Work begins on the Seikan Tunnel in Japan.

1959
Britain's first motorway opens between London and Birmingham.

1964
The Chesapeake Tunnel Bridge opens on the Atlantic coast of the USA.

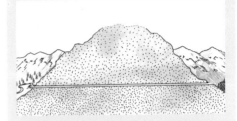

1965
The Mont Blanc Road Tunnel opens between France and Italy.

1975
The Henderson Tunnel in Colorado opens. It is 15.8 km long and is the USA's longest railway tunnel.

1982
St Gotthard Rail Tunnel opens in Switzerland. The tunnel has taken ten years to complete.

1987
Work begins on the Channel Tunnel between England and France. A tunnel was first suggested by Napoleon in 1802.

1988
Japan's Seikan Tunnel finally opens, after 42 years' work.

1994
The Channel Tunnel opens. The journey across the Channel takes 35 minutes.

From start to finish

On these two pages, you can follow the Step by Step stories in the bottom right-hand corner of each double page from start to finish.

BUILDING A ROAD TUNNEL

1 Before a tunnel is planned, geologists dig boreholes to find out what kind of ground lies on the route.

2 Once they are ready to start work, geologists examine the rockface closely to find out where to place explosives.

3 The exact positions chosen for the explosives are put onto computer disc at offices away from the tunnel site.

4 The disc is loaded into a computer on a drilling jumbo. The jumbo then automatically drills holes in the correct places.

5 When all the holes have been made, they are filled with powerful explosives. The engineers know exactly how much explosive to use.

6 An electric detonator is used to set the explosives off. The explosion removes slices of rock along the tunnel route.

7 When all the dust and smoke has cleared, bulldozers pick up the rock fragments produced by the explosion.

8 The waste material, called muck or spoil, is loaded into large dumper trucks and carried out of the new tunnel.

9 This process is repeated many times to build a complete tunnel. To save time, long tunnels are often built from both ends.

10 Shafts are sometimes drilled down to the tunnel so that work can carry on in several places at the same time.

11 Engineers use laser beams to check that the work is on course and that the two tunnels will meet in the middle.

12 The new tunnel is lined with steel mesh to keep small pieces of rock from falling and to strengthen the tunnel walls.

13 Next the mesh is sprayed with layers of liquid concrete called shotcrete. This prevents water seeping into the tunnel.

14 When the tunnellers working from each end meet one another, they know that the toughest work is over.

15 Once a road tunnel has been completed and lined, road-building can begin. The roadbed goes down first.

16 Road-laying machines lay the road surface. The road-paver spreads the tarmac and the road-roller flattens down the surface.

17 Teams of workers move in to instal emergency telephones, lights, and air-conditioning. Cat's-eyes are embedded into the road.

18 Before the road tunnel can be opened, it is checked thoroughly by engineers to make sure it is safe to use.

Glossary

aggregate Broken and crushed stone used in roadmaking. The foundation of a road is usually made up of two layers of aggregate.

borehole A hole drilled into the ground to obtain samples of soil and rock from beneath the surface.

cambered The slight upward curve to the centre of the surface of a road, which helps water to drain away to the sides.

caravan A group of traders or other people travelling together for safety through the desert.

carriageway The part of a road along which traffic travels in one direction only.

central reservation The raised surface, sometimes with a crash barrier, which separates traffic moving in opposite directions.

compress To make firm by flattening and rolling.

cut-and-cover A method of building tunnels by cutting an open trench, building the tunnel inside it and then covering it with earth.

cutting A trench cut through high ground to carry a road, avoiding steep slopes.

drift mine A coal mine made by digging a horizontal tunnel into the side of a hill.

drilling jumbo A very large drilling machine mounted on wheels or tracks. A drilling jumbo can drill many holes at the same time.

dual carriageway A road on which traffic moving in opposite directions is separated by markings or a **central reservation.**

embankment An artificial slope built to avoid sharp climbs or drops.

Etruscans People who created a civilisation in northern Italy between the twelfth and fourth centuries BC.

excavate To remove soil by digging down into the ground.

exit ramp A sloping lane which carries traffic from one road to another.

Federal Paid for by central United States Government funds rather than by individual state governments.

flyover An overhead road which carries fast traffic over less important roads.

gelignite A waterproof explosive used in blasting operations, invented by Alfred Nobel in 1887.

geological survey A study of the soil and rocks lying on and below a piece of land.

geologist A scientist who studies rocks and soil.

hydraulic jack A device which raises heavy loads and objects using hydraulic power. To make a jack work, fluid is pumped into a cylinder, which pushes a piston in the cylinder upwards .

interchange The arrangement of roads which enables traffic to move between major roads.

intersection The point at which two major roads meet or cross.

junction The place where two or more roads meet, link or cross each other.

muck Material, such as soil or rock ,which is dug out during the building of a road or tunnel.

Middle Ages In Europe, the period from the end of the Roman empire in the fifth century AD to the Italian Renaissance in the fifteenth century.

pier A strong pillar which supports a structure such as a bridge or **flyover**.

pile A steel or concrete column reaching down to solid rock under layers of soft soil to give support for a structure.

pre-stressed A method of strengthening structural concrete by sealing stretched steel cables inside it.

seams Underground bands of coal sandwiched between other rocks.

sediment Sand and other soft material found on the bed of seas and rivers.

sewage Waste liquids which are carried away from homes, factories and other building to be treated.

shaft A vertical opening dug in the ground to reach coal beneath the surface.

shotcrete Liquid cement which is sprayed on to the lining of a tunnel to form a waterproof barrier.

slip roads Short roads which carry traffic entering or leaving a major road.

spoil Like **muck,** material which is dug out when a road or tunnel is built.

spur roads Roads forming part of a layout which carries traffic between different roads, or a short side road leading off a main road.

sub-soil The rocks or other material beneath the surface of the ground.

surveyor A professional who examines land, both on maps and on the ground, in order to plan the route of a road.

survey station A building containing instruments and large-scale maps which enable **surveyors** to check that road works are going according to plan. The checks are continued until the road is completed.

tension The pulling apart and stretching of an object.

terracotta Clay fired in a kiln to make it hard.

terrain The piece of land over which a road is to be built.

theodolite An instrument containing a telescope for measuring horizontal and vertical angles, used by **surveyors.**

Trench warfare A type of warfare used in the First World War in which opposing armies faced each other from their positions in the trenches.

weld To join two pieces of metal by melting their edges and forcing them together, or by adding molten metal between them.

Index

Words in **bold** appear in the glossary on pages 46 and 47.